A Walk Thru the Life of

ABRAHAM

Faith in God's Promises

Walk Thru the Bible

BakerBooks
a division of Baker Publishing Group
Grand Rapids, Michigan

Published by Baker Books
a division of Baker Publishing Group
P.O. Box 6287, Grand Rapids, MI 49516-6287
www.bakerbooks.com

Printed in the United States of America

Library of Congress Cataloging-in-Publication Data
A walk thru the life of Abraham : faith in God's promises / Walk Thru the Bible.
    p. cm.
Includes bibliographical references (p.   ).
ISBN 978-0-8010-7178-2 (pbk.)
1. Abraham (Biblical patriarch) 2. Bible. O.T. Genesis XII–XXV, 11—Text-books. I. Walk Thru the Bible (Educational ministry)
BS580.A3W26 2010
222′.11092—dc22   2009046942

10 11 12 13 14 15 16   7 6 5 4 3 2 1

Contents

Introduction 5

Session 1 Chosen 11
Session 2 Challenges 19
Session 3 Faith and Action 26
Session 4 Faith and Friendship 34
Session 5 Fulfillment 42
Session 6 An Epic Test 49

Conclusion 59
Leader's Notes 61
Bibliography 63

Introduction

It was a desperate attempt at some semblance of immortality. Long before a pharaoh died, the construction of his tomb would begin. Passages and compartments within the pyramid would be designed for maximum security to throw grave robbers off track. The mummification process would protect the king's body and organs against decay for centuries to come. Helpful items—statues of laborers, scrolls of magic spells, boats for travel—would be placed in the inner chambers to assist the dead king in the afterlife. And the pyramid itself would stand practically forever as a monument to the king's grandeur. It was as close to an eternal legacy as a human being could get.

Most Egyptian pyramids had already been built long before Abraham was born. But the nomad from Ur ended up with a legacy far greater, far more lasting than anything the pharaohs ever dreamed of. How? Not by conquering kingdoms, building monuments, or exploring new lands, but by living a life of faith in response to a God who chose him from among masses of other men. Simply by entering a covenant with this God, the otherwise unremarkable sojourner and his descendants impacted billions of people throughout history. Abraham became the vehicle through whom God would reveal himself to humanity in specific, tangible ways.

His story is a model for anyone who wants to leave a legacy and make a lasting difference in the world. The way to impact the history of an eternal kingdom is to enter into a covenant with the eternal God. And the only way to do that is by faith. Those who accept the revealed truth of God and live accordingly, regardless of what they see with their eyes, become a part of the family of the wandering Aramean named Abraham.

Abraham

As the story goes, a craftsman named Terah made idols. His oldest son, Abram, began having doubts about all the gods worshiped by the people of his culture. So one time when his father was out, Abram smashed all the idols in the family's shop except the largest one, then put a stick in the hands of the one remaining statue. When his father came back, he was furious. But Abram blamed the vandalism on the standing idol, who had gotten angry at all the smaller statues. His father accused him of lying on the obvious grounds that idols can't speak or move—to which Abram responded, "Then why do you worship them?"

This rabbinic tale and others like it are fanciful attempts to explain why God chose this particular man out of multitudes of others in a polytheistic society. In truth, we have no information about anything that went on in Abraham's life before God called him to leave home and go to a land of promise. We have no indication that Abraham was monotheistic before God spoke to him (see Josh. 24:2), or even that he was monotheistic for some time afterward. God didn't give him a theology; he gave him a command. In obedience, Abraham left the polytheism of Mesopotamia and entered a relationship with one God whom he would learn about in a series of experiences over many years.

We don't know exactly when Abraham lived. Most estimates place him sometime between 2000 and 1800 BC. His family originally came from Ur, but even that isn't very specific. A large city on the Euphrates called Ur was a prosperous, highly developed area with spacious homes and a relatively high standard of living. Much farther north was a smaller city called Ur about which little is known. Most scholars assume that the family migrated to Haran from the larger, southern Ur, but no one knows for sure. Regardless, we know Abraham was in Haran when his adventure with God began.

Abraham's life is neatly divided. He lived seventy-five years before his call and before the promise of a son and descendants was given; twenty-five interim years between the promise and its fulfillment; and seventy-five years after Isaac's birth. The middle twenty-five years—plus the somewhat later offering of Isaac—are the key focus of the Genesis story. During these years, Abraham wrestled with God's purposes, exhibited great faith, sometimes expressed doubts, made some mistakes, and drew closer to the God who had called him. As this divine-human relationship unfolded, Abraham became God's friend— so designated in much later writings (2 Chron. 20:7; Isa. 41:8; James 2:23).

Themes

Up to this point, the history of God's dealings with humanity had been on a grand scale; after the exile from Eden come stories of the great flood and the tower of Babel, both large-scale judgments. With Abraham, salvation history zeroed in on one man and his family, which grew into a people, then a nation, and finally, through a Messiah, spread over the entire world. And it was all made possible because one very human nomad became a friend of God. Abraham became the hinge between macro- and micro-history, between the general and the particular revelation of God.

We can learn a lot about God's purposes by the themes that show up in Abraham's life. It's significant that his story begins with barrenness and wandering—perfect conditions for a God who wants to make extravagant promises of descendants and land. In fact, barrenness becomes a recurring theme in Scripture. After Sarah came Rebekah, Rachel, Samson's mother, Hannah, and, in the New Testament, Elizabeth. What better way for a God of hope to demonstrate his love and his power than to step into hopeless situations? This is what he does again and again, and it starts with Abraham and his wife.

Such hardships are the stage on which God's promises are best displayed. Perhaps the dominant theme of Abraham's life is faith. He becomes "exhibit A" for how God chooses to deal with human beings. God establishes covenants and invites his people into them in such a way that they can only relate to him by faith. Abraham's life is a decades-long case study in this truth. That's why God's promises are reiterated so often in Abraham's life and why Abraham is stripped of all human possibilities for realizing those promises. To qualify as a patriarch in the kingdom of God, he must learn to trust God radically and exclusively. In so doing, he becomes an eternal prototype of God's relationship with human beings.

One thing we learn from Abraham through all of his experiences with God is that it isn't easy being chosen. God's people have found that to be true throughout history. But it's far better than the alternative. The privilege of walking with

God, even when the path is painful, is always worth the effort. The blessings that come to Abraham—and then through him to the world—make that abundantly clear.

How to Use This Guide

The discussion guides in this series are intended to create a link between past and present, between the cultural and historical context of the Bible and real life as we experience it today. By putting ourselves as closely into biblical situations as possible, we can begin to understand how God interacted with his people in the past and, therefore, how he interacts with us today. The information in this book makes ancient Scripture relevant to twenty-first-century life as God means for us to live it.

The questions in this book are geared to do what a discussion guide should do: provoke discussion. You won't see obvious "right" answers to most of these questions. That's because biblical characters had to wrestle with deep spiritual issues and didn't have easy, black-and-white answers handed to them. They discovered God's will as he led them and revealed himself to them—the same process we go through today, though we have the added help of their experiences to inform us. Biblical characters experienced God in complex situations, and so do we. By portraying those situations realistically, we learn how to apply the Bible to our own lives. One of the best ways to do that is through in-depth discussion with other believers.

The discussion questions within each session are designed to elicit every participant's input, regardless of his or her level of preparation. Obviously, the more group members prepare by reading the biblical text and the background information in the study guide, the more they will get out of it. But even in busy weeks that afford no preparation time, everyone will be able to participate in a meaningful way.

The discussion questions also allow your group quite a bit of latitude. Some groups prefer to briefly discuss the questions in order to cover as many as possible, while others focus only on one or two of them in order to have more in-depth conversations. Since this study is designed for flexibility, feel free to adapt it according to the personality and needs of your group.

Each session ends with a hypothetical situation that relates to the passage of the week. Discussion questions are provided, but group members may also want to consider role-playing the scenario or setting up a two-team debate over one or two of the questions. These exercises often cultivate insights that wouldn't come out of a typical discussion.

Regardless of how you use this material, the biblical text will always be the ultimate authority. Your discussions may take you to many places and cover many issues, but they will have the greatest impact when they begin and end with God's Word itself. And never forget that the Spirit who inspired the Word is in on the discussion too. May he guide it—and you—wherever he wishes.

Chosen

GENESIS 12

They had left the homeland bound for Canaan, but they stopped and settled down before they arrived. That often happens in life—you set out with one goal in mind, and then your goal gets redefined along the way. There's no shame in that. But Scripture gives the impression that Terah's family didn't just settle down; they settled. Stopped short. Compromised. As Genesis 11 closes, they have put down roots in an in-between place.

We don't know much about what that was like for Abram, the oldest son in Terah's family. We know his family worshiped a variety of gods (Josh. 24:2). Who didn't? The world was polytheistic. That's what people did. And we know that the gods hadn't shown Abram much favor, at least in the hugely important area of leaving a legacy. Abram was seventy-five and childless. His wife was barren—a profound crisis for a man of his time. According to the laws of his society, Abram could have divorced her, impregnated a household slave girl in her place, or hired a prostitute to carry his child. But there's no indication that he even considered such action. Instead, he lived without expectations of a legacy, seemingly destined to leave his inheritance to a nephew or a servant. Lingering somewhere between his past home and his original goals, he was a man without prospects.

If we're honest, that's where many of us live. We're somewhere between where we started out and where we're going, and we tend to settle down—or settle for less than what we had hoped for. We suspect that God may have something else in store for us, but we don't know how to get there. So we lower our expectations, compromise our dreams, and consent to the status quo. We think the in-between land is all we have, so we try to get comfortable in it.

Abram is a symbol of a life that has grown stagnant and perhaps restless. We don't know that he actually felt that way—the Bible is silent about his beliefs and attitudes before God called him. For all we know, he was dreaming of doing something great or expecting a miracle. But that isn't how Scripture portrays him. We aren't told why God singled him out above all his peers. All we're told is that God chose a member of a migrant family who was just about past the age of hoping. And that choice would change the world forever.

The Call: Genesis 12:1–9

Seemingly out of nowhere, God speaks, and his message is radical. Abram is to leave his family home and go to a place that God will reveal later. His father is about 145 at this time and will live sixty more years; that's how the chronology adds

REVERSING THE CURSE

In Genesis 3, God exiled Adam and Eve from Eden, multiplied the pain of childbirth, cursed the ground so that it would produce food only through hard labor, and subjected human beings to death. God's promises to Abram don't completely reverse those curses, but they do begin to address them positively. Instead of exile, Abram and Sarai are promised a land. In contrast to the pain of childbirth, they are promised the joy of having a child and many descendants. Instead of hard, futile toil, they are promised abundance. And instead of the finality of death, they are promised a lasting legacy that will bless the entire earth.

up, even though his eventual death was reported at the end of chapter 11. So Abram isn't just venturing out on his own. He's leaving behind everything—his inheritance, the protection afforded by the family's gods, his means of provision, and his security—to follow God into the unknown. He takes along his wife Sarai, his nephew Lot, and a substantial entourage of servants he has acquired over the years, but this is essentially a divorce from his ancestral past and a denial of any predictable future. And in taking Lot with him, he is also taking Terah's only grandchild. In many families, this breach of expectations would be an affront. In Abram's, it's a divine calling.

But it's a calling that comes with astounding promises: he will become a great nation, he will be blessed, his name will be magnified, he will bless others, those who honor him will be blessed, those who dishonor him will be cursed, and all the families of the earth will be blessed through him. And just in case he misheard, these promises will be repeated and emphasized again and again—to Abram in Genesis 15 and 17, and to his grandson Jacob in Genesis 28. God is serious about this plan.

Needless to say, migrating by God's invisible hand will require some adjustments. God hasn't laid out a detailed blueprint for Abram but has simply given him an initial command and a big-picture promise. The details will be a matter of trial and error over the next few decades. And the land he will settle in—God eventually specifies Canaan in 12:7, after Abram comes into it—is unfamiliar. Its hills, especially in the north, slow down travel. Its people may be hospitable to those who pass through, but those who come to stay often encounter resistance. It's easy for an outsider to get caught between tribal rivalries or fall victim to plundering. The land is good, but it isn't entirely welcoming. It may take a lot of time before a sojourner can call it home.

Even so, Abram sets up altars within the land. This voice that called him, this God that has reached out in a way that other gods don't, is worthy of his worship. Abram will stake his claim to the land with altars at Shechem, Bethel, Hebron, and eventually a mountain of Moriah—sites that will become sacred in the course of Israel's history. Though he is in unfamiliar territory, he begins to mark it for the God who called him there.

Discuss

- Why do you think God didn't tell Abram up front where he would be going? Why do you think God didn't extend the invitation to the entire family—Abram's father and brothers included?

_____

_____

_____

_____

• In what ways is this very first experience between God and Abram representative of everyone's experience with God throughout history? In what ways can you relate to Abram's calling?

_____

_____

_____

_____

A Diversion: Genesis 12:10–20

There's a famine in Canaan, and Abram is faced with a choice: stay in the land God has just designated as his inheritance or leave that land to feed the family. He chooses to leave. Is it because he doubts God's ability to provide in the land of promise?

SARAI'S BEAUTY

Twice in Genesis, Abram fears that Sarai's beauty will attract unwelcome attention from rulers looking to expand their harems. This poses somewhat of a problem for interpreters because Sarai was in her late sixties in the first episode and in her late eighties in the second. It's hard for Bible commentators to imagine her being irresistible to kings whose harems were filled with twenty-year-olds. There are several potential explanations, however. It's certainly possible that Sarai supernaturally retained her youthful beauty; after all, she was supernaturally rejuvenated to bear a child at the age of ninety. She may have also been beautiful for her dignity or for having a regal demeanor. And because many references in Genesis seem to point to Abram's status as a powerful tribal chieftain, she may have been highly attractive as relationship collateral, for her wealth, and for a variety of other reasons. But these latter explanations can only be part of the story, as the text insists that she was more than just attractive. She was very beautiful.

15

Or is it an act of faith that he will be brought back in due time? The text doesn't say for sure, but it does hint at compromise. Throughout Scripture, Egypt is symbolic of living by sight rather than by faith, of depending on human strength rather than on God. And Abram and Sarai do encounter difficulty there. The promise of descendants is immediately threatened by the prospect of Sarai being taken into Pharaoh's harem.

A savvy traveler, Abram has a policy of telling powerful kings that his beautiful wife is really his sister. Technically it's true—he spells this policy out in 20:12–13 when the situation comes up again—but it's a risky strategy. His options are to (1) truthfully say that Sarai is his wife and trust God to protect them both—though if God doesn't, he will be killed and his wife will be taken into the king's harem; or (2) semi-truthfully say that Sarai is his sister, in which case Abram's life will be spared and she will be taken into the king's harem anyway. He chooses the latter, the less gallant option, and finds that God protects them both. Pharaoh even sends them away with parting gifts. God is apparently watching over his promise.

The scene foreshadows a much greater exodus to come. Abram's beloved is held tightly in the grip of a pharaoh, God sends plagues on the Egyptians, and the beloved is released—with added wealth. More than five hundred years later this scenario will be played out again on a grander scale as God rescues his people from slavery in Egypt. But in Abram's case, what could have been a rape and murder in the worst-case scenario turned into a blessing and greater wealth. It's the first time God's promise is threatened, but it won't be the last.

Discuss

- Do you think the famine was a test to see if Abram would stay in the land that had been promised to him? Why or why not? In what ways have you found God's promises tested in your life? How have you been tempted to compromise them?

_____

_____

_____

_____

- In what ways did God demonstrate his protection of Abram and Sarai? To what degree do you think his protection was dependent on their making the right choices?

_____

_____

_____

_____

A CASE STUDY

Imagine: Several years ago, you got a new job and moved to a new city along with your family. Only now is it beginning to feel like home, and even though it isn't the perfect situation—after all, there's probably no such thing—you feel that you could grow roots here and live out the rest of your days. But God suddenly intervenes in your life with an irresistible and growing conviction that you're called to do a greater work somewhere else. When your family asks you what the work is and where you're supposed to go, all you can tell them is that you don't know. You only know that you're supposed to uproot and begin driving in the one direction you've never been before. Only then will God give you more specifics.

- How certain would you be that your conviction is God's voice? Do you think he would really tell you something so disruptive and inconvenient? What would you say to him about the lack of specifics he has given you?
- How do you think your friends and family would react to your sense of calling? Would any of them be supportive? Would any of them try to talk you out of it?
- In what ways, if any, does this scenario reflect the life of faith for everyone?

Challenges

GENESIS 13–14

Looking back over her life, she wondered if she had missed it—whatever "it" was. Destiny, perhaps? Or maybe "it" was God's will, her original design, or the dreams she had always longed for. Whatever. She had taken so many detours, made so many mistakes, suffered so often from others' mistakes, that any semblance of design or destiny was surely lost in the distant past. Long ago she heard that God had a wonderful plan for her life. But oh, how that plan had been assaulted. Circumstances conspired against it. She had been tempted to stray from it, distracted from following it, and even confused about what the plan was in the first place. Now she just doubted. The "wonderful plan" had been a nice thought, but she was almost certain she was too far off track.

That describes a lot of people. It might even describe Abram several times in his story. After all, he's pushing eighty at the end of Genesis 12, and he may have already made a misstep on his new venture with God. There will be more of those too—some minor, others sending out ripples for centuries to come. The only thing holding God's promise together through most of his story is ... well, God. Persistent, outright rebellion may cause many to miss out on his plan, but mistakes? Temporary lapses of judgment? Uncertainty about what the plan is? No, not when God has committed to fulfill his purposes in someone's life. The One who promised is the One who watches over his promises.

That's important to know as we go through the twists and turns of life. Sometimes those twists and turns are self-inflicted, and sometimes they are the product of circumstances beyond our control. Either way, when we remain faithful—and often even when we don't—the hand of God's sovereignty keeps pulling us back into his purposes.

Abram and Sarai experience God's sovereign care in this session as the promise has to endure an unwitting decision by Abram and Lot, an attack on a fringe portion of the land, and a temptation to get the land in the wrong way at the wrong time. They are still following God the best way they know how. Their path is imprecise, imperfect, and unpredictable. But God is there, guiding them, protecting them, and building character and faith. He is making his servants into the people he wants them to be.

Abram the Compliant: Genesis 13

By now Abram is very wealthy, so he returns to Canaan with Sarai and Lot. He returns to the altar he had once erected near Bethel—as if to recommit to remaining in the land of God's promise. But soon there is conflict between his shepherds and Lot's. Grazing land is sparse during dry season, so it's only natural, with expanding herds and nearby native clans, that space

LOT REVISITED

Lot is typically portrayed as making a selfish choice when he selects the fertile valley along the Jordan. While that portrayal may be true, his actions aren't as overtly selfish as they seem. Either he or Abraham could have gone to the Jordan valley long before this agreement was made, but neither had. Why? Perhaps because the valley was fruitful for only part of the year, but the hill country was more desirable year-round. And Lot essentially volunteered to be the one to move, allowing his uncle to remain where he already was—which could be perceived as a selfless act. But Scripture does seem to hint that Lot based his choice on immediate appeal rather than long-term wisdom. Whether selfish or not, he represents a larger biblical theme: in the long run, those who live by sight enjoy fewer blessings than those who, like Abram, live by faith.

would become a little cramped. So Abram proposes a solution: an amicable separation with a clear division of land. The suggestion demonstrates a shift in his thinking. Only recently he had taken matters into his own hands to find productive land in Egypt; now he willingly offers his nephew the land described as being "like the land of Egypt."

Lot sees the fertile Jordan valley, and not only is it like Egypt, it's "like the garden of the LORD" (13:10), so he chooses it. Once again, God is preserving his promise to Abram; Lot could have chosen the land God has already designated as belonging to Abram's descendants. Does Abram allow that option because he still thinks his inheritance will pass to a relative such as Lot? Perhaps. For some time to come, he will express confusion about who the heir of a childless man could possibly be. Regardless, God is guiding the promise to fulfillment, even though it's still beyond Abram's comprehension.

Lot moves into his new land and pitches his tents near a city steeped in evil—a choice he will one day regret. Again God emphasizes his promise to Abram for countless offspring and a homeland forever. *This* land. Not Egypt, not the land Lot just chose, but the land Abram almost gave away. All of Canaan will be his. So Abram builds an altar in the center of Canaan—in Hebron, a significant city used as a Canaanite capital—and worships.

Discuss

- How clearly did Abram see God's promises for his life? Why do you think God let him live with his misunderstandings?

  _____

  _____

  _____

  _____

- How clearly do you see God's promises for your life? What do you wish God would spell out for you? Why do you think he hasn't?

  _____

  _____

  _____

  _____

Abram the Warrior: Genesis 14

Focus: Genesis 14:17–24

A menacing coalition gathers and attacks the five cities of the plain where Lot now lives. They come from the east—one of them rules where the tower of Babel had been built—and their names are loaded with connotations of pride, rebellion, blindness, and dread. They come by the same route Abram had taken when he left the homeland, almost as if an enemy of God's plan is chasing after the promise. But they don't attack Abram; they clash in a valley of tar pits, sack Sodom and four other cities of the plain, steal their wealth, and take the people captive. Among their captives is the nephew of God's chosen servant. Something has to be done.

Abram musters his small army of fighting men and pursues the enemy far into the north. In a night attack, he defeats the coalition. But that isn't enough; he pursues the kings even further, chasing them far out of the land of promise. Then he frees the captives and restores their wealth.

The battle sets the stage for one of the most peculiar encounters in Scripture. Out of nowhere, a priest of the Most High God appears. Melchizedek is said to be the king of Salem—

THE MYSTERY OF MELCHIZEDEK

Melchizedek appears out of nowhere—no genealogy, no recorded birth or death, no clear geographic origin. His name means "King of Righteousness," and he is the ruler of Salem—literally, the "king of peace." He's also "a priest of God Most High." He serves Abram a highly symbolic meal of bread and wine, blesses him in the name of God, and receives Abram's offering. A psalm of David will later refer to the Messiah as a priest forever according to the order of Melchizedek (Ps. 110:4). It's no wonder, then, that the New Testament picks up on Melchizedek as a Christ figure (Hebrews 5–7), and that many Bible interpreters throughout church history see Genesis 14 as an appearance of the preincarnate Messiah. Melchizedek is, at the very least, a prophetic picture of Jesus.

presumably Jerusalem, though the city hasn't yet been built. At best, it's a small settlement under another name. But he comes with an effusive blessing that validates Abram's special status before God. Abram receives the blessing, shares a highly symbolic meal with him, and offers him a tenth of the spoils of war.

Then Abram encounters the recently rescued king of Sodom, who offers him all the wealth regained in the battle. And he is in a perfect position now to claim the land God has promised. He has demonstrated his power and the region owes him a huge debt. But Abram refuses. He will not be debtor to any king in this land of promise. It is God, and God alone, who establishes him.

Discuss

- What do Abram's actions—the counterattack, the far-reaching pursuit, and the devotion to a priest-king sent from God—say about his faith at this point in his life?

  _____

  _____

  _____

  _____

- Abram had a perfect opportunity to exert his power over the region and to realize God's promise that he would possess the land. Why do you think he didn't see that opportunity as God's plan?

  _____

  _____

  _____

  _____

A Case Study

Imagine: You've been praying for an opportunity in a new line of work—a field you have felt called to for some time. In fact, you're convinced that God has confirmed your sense of calling with quite a few promises from his Word. So when you receive an out-of-the-blue offer in that field and have a chance to embark on your new career, it certainly seems like God is opening doors. The only problem is that you'll have to relocate, which you didn't expect; and in order to do that, you'll need to go into more debt than you're comfortable with. But God often works in unexpected ways, and though this isn't shaping up exactly as you thought it would, it does seem like an answer to prayer.

- What aspects of this opportunity make it seem like it's from God? What aspects might cause you to wonder if it is? How can you know whether this is an answer to prayer?
- Do you think God normally fulfills his promises in ways that we expect he will? Why or why not?
- What criteria do you use to determine whether an open door is from God or not?

Faith and Action

GENESIS 15–16

George Müller was certain that God had called him to the mission field. So he left the kingdom of Prussia and moved to England to work with the London Missionary Society. He hoped to venture into more distant fields on other continents, but his dreams never materialized. He became a pastor of a church and founded orphanages that ministered to thousands of young people over several decades. Finally, at the age of seventy, he began a seventeen-year period of missionary travel that allowed him to minister in over forty countries on several continents. He became a prominent leader of the missionary movement.

At what point in his life was Müller a missionary? In some ways, he always was, but not in the way he expected. His dreams of foreign service didn't materialize until he was to the age when most men retire. He had always tried to follow God's call, but God's call didn't always work out the way he thought it would. Even so, God directed him at every turn, even when Müller made mistakes—or at least what he considered to be mistakes. What began as a general promise grew more specific over time, and a life of fruitfulness was the result.

That's usually how God's call works. We have a tendency to view Abram as receiving a very specific, clear promise and then being impatient and doubtful while he waited long years for it to be fulfilled. The truth is that the promise began in general terms and got more specific over time. God clarified and refined it after Abram's missteps and misperceptions. Like the rest of us, Abram wrestled with God's purposes and knew that God could fulfill them in a variety of ways. Some of his assumptions—that the descendants might come through his servant or through a surrogate mother—were realistic, a product of thinking that God usually works within natural, normal parameters in our lives.

We can hardly blame Abram for that. We all think that way. An infertile couple today might assume that God's provision for them is adoption rather than defying medical odds and making them physically able to have a child. They may be exactly right—or God may do an unexpected miracle. A person in financial crisis might assume God will deliver through the normal means of hard work and a lot of time. And that might be exactly right too—or God may provide a sudden, unexpected windfall through highly unusual means. We waver between hoping for a supernatural miracle and expecting a "normal," realistic miracle. Why? Because we know God does both—sometimes the former, usually the latter. But both are always real possibilities.

27

That's why we have competing voices in our lives and sometimes even within our own heads. Some voices remind us to be realistic, to remember that faith isn't a matter of turning off our brains, to observe how God normally works in our lives. Other voices remind us that the Bible is full of supernatural events, dramatic deliverances, and mind-boggling miracles. Most of us live between the tension, knowing that God will intervene and fulfill his promises but wondering exactly how. That's where Abram lived for twenty-five years, and God called it "faith."

The Promise Sealed: Genesis 15

God comes to Abram in a dream and speaks the first "do not fear" in Scripture. Has Abram been afraid? We don't know, but time is passing and the promise of descendants is not yet being fulfilled. Abram wonders—will it be fulfilled through his servant Eliezer? There's a hint of disappointment, maybe even accusation in his question. "You have given me no children," he reminds God, so the only obvious option is to leave his inheritance to

RECKONED AS RIGHTEOUSNESS

Genesis 15:6 became a foundational verse in the theology of the early church, especially in Paul's writings. To Paul, it proved that righteousness comes through faith, apart from the law (Rom. 3:28), since the law came centuries after Abraham's time. This verse is quoted and discussed extensively in Romans 4–5 and Galatians 3:6–14. James uses it too, but for a different reason: to point out that Abraham's righteousness, which came by faith alone, also resulted in works of faith (James 2:23). This kind of faith—the faith that justifies us but also produces righteousness in us—is the kind that, according to James, makes someone a friend of God.

28

an adopted heir. But God isn't dependent on obvious options. The promise of many descendants is reiterated more specifically this time: "a son coming from your own body" (15:4).

The assurance of the old promise comes after the announcement of an even more significant promise, though Abram hardly seems to notice: "I am your shield, your very great reward" (15:1). Some translations say "your reward will be great," but the literal implication here is that God is the reward. It's a personal commitment; God isn't just giving Abram a son, many descendants, and land. He's giving Abram himself. Abram's focus at this point is clearly on the gifts rather than the Giver, though that focus will shift and be dramatically tested later. Over time, Abram will learn that knowing God as a great Reward is better than experiencing him as a great Rewarder.

Abram has already received the promise of land in earlier chapters, but his question this time seems to come from a heart that thinks it has waited far too long. "How can I know?" (15:8). This from a man who, just two verses earlier, "believed the LORD, and he credited it to him as righteousness." Many centuries later a priest named Zechariah will ask this same question about a promise made to him and be rebuked for it (Luke 1:18–20), but Abram doesn't have the benefit of recorded Scripture to assure him of God's faithfulness. God is patient with him. In fact, God initiates a remarkable ceremony to seal the covenant.

The ritual of splitting animals and passing through them wasn't unusual in Mesopotamian culture; it expressed commitment to a pact, as if each party were saying, "May I be likewise torn apart if I break this covenant." But the manner in which this covenant is effected is highly unusual. For one thing, it's an unprecedented contract between a deity and a human. And unlike most covenants, God secures this one himself, unilaterally, after immobilizing Abram in a deep sleep. The deity is active

29

and the human is passive. Fire pierces the dark of night, the Lord utters a somber prophecy, and the agreement is sealed. It's a sacred ceremony, and its terms are irrevocable. God has promised, and he will carry it out.

Discuss

- Do you think Abram sinned by asking how he could know for certain whether a promise God had already spoken several times was true? Why or why not?

  _____

  _____

  _____

  _____

- What do you think is the significance of God's unilateral covenant? What can Abram do to fulfill it? What can he do to disqualify himself from it?

  _____

  _____

  _____

  _____

The Promise Misunderstood: Genesis 16

To this point, God has not said that Abram's descendants will come through Sarai, and Abram hasn't asked. And since Sarai has always been barren and is now old, God apparently has other means. So Abram listens when Sarai offers her maid, Hagar, as a surrogate. It's a reasonable offer from someone raised in a culture in which barren women are often required by law to find an alternate mother for their husband's children. God has

THE QUEST FOR AN HEIR

In all ancient Near Eastern cultures, the need for a son to carry on the family name and inheritance and to establish a father's legacy was enormously important. This is clearly spelled out in the various legal codes from Abraham's time. Cuneiform tablets have revealed a widespread practice of couples adopting someone to be the family's "son" in the absence of a biological son. The adoptee could be anyone, but was usually a respected servant of the family. This was seen as a last resort, though Abram mentions it before he and Sarai attempted the more common means of finding a surrogate. In several nearby cultures, an infertile wife was required by law to find someone to bear her husband's children. The children would then officially belong to the main wife, not the concubine—which is apparently how Sarai expected things to work with the son of Hagar, until the friction arising from such an arrangement became understandably unbearable.

made it clear that he wants Abram to have a son. Since Sarai's womb is closed, this plan makes sense.

The Egyptian girl conceives; it seems the promise is being fulfilled. Perhaps she is exalted in her own eyes, seeing herself as the special instrument through whom God is fulfilling his extravagant plans for Abram. Whatever the reason, Hagar shows contempt for Sarai, the barren one, the one God has obviously not chosen to use for his purposes. And Sarai can hardly stand it.

Sarai deals harshly with Hagar, banishing her into the wilderness. But God has mercy. The Egyptian is, after all, carrying a son of Abram, whose future offspring has already been blessed. She and her child will not be left out of God's promises. In a tender expression of his care, God reassures Hagar, gives her a blessing and a prophecy about her son's descendants, names the child Ishmael—"God hears"—and

31

sends her back home. Her testimony from the desert must carry some weight. Abram does name the child Ishmael, as God had said, and for the next thirteen years, Hagar and her son will live under the roof of the mistress who had banished them.

Discuss

- Abram and Sarai may have thought they were stepping out in faith when they were really stepping out on an assumption. How can we discern the difference between those two things? When does God want us to passively wait for a promise, and when does he want us to actively take initiative toward it?

  _____

  _____

  _____

  _____

A Case Study

Imagine: For years, you've prayed for God to meet your deepest desire for a very tangible gift. It's a longing so personal that you can hardly tell anyone about it, but you know it's from God. He has promised to fulfill this desire; you're certain of that. But time passes, and your longing grows deeper and more painful. You yearn for the fulfillment, watching your circumstances carefully for any sign of his provision. Finally, Jesus shows up in your living room one day and tells you that he's here to stay. And he has an announcement to make: "I _am_ your reward. I _am_ your fulfillment. I _am_ what you long for."

- To what extent does this announcement satisfy or fulfill you? Are you worried that the gift of Jesus's presence is meant to replace the tangible blessing you sought? Or do you immediately think, "Yes, Lord, you're all I need"? Why?
- In all honesty, which gets more attention in your prayer life: the gifts or the Giver? Why?
- In what ways does God meet our needs with himself? In what ways does he meet our needs with his gifts?

Faith and Friendship

GENESIS 17–18

If an older couple—gray-haired, wrinkled, at least in their eighties—showed up at church on Sunday and said they were still holding onto a promise for a child, a wise pastor or staff member would refer them for counseling services. The absurdity of their hope would be considered pathological, not faithful. Yet repeatedly throughout Scripture, God promises impossible things. He portrays himself as a deliverer, a rescuer, a provider, a healer, and more—and he always seems to set the stage with extreme situations to make his intervention all the more remarkable. The impossibilities of Scripture highlight his power to overcome them. He is by nature a promiser of extraordinary capabilities.

How can we know when someone's faith is godly and when it is ludicrous? If Scripture is our guide, we usually can't—not before God proves it or denies it. The truth is that God calls his people to follow him with bold, audacious faith that can often look absurd to observers. The problem is that sometimes people believe absurd things that God didn't put in their hearts. Human eyes have a hard time telling the difference. Only God can vindicate a true believer.

God vindicated Abram and Sarai, but they probably endured plenty of skeptics along the slow and excruciating way. Perhaps that's one reason God waited so long to fulfill his promise of a son—to give their faith plenty of time to season and grow strong in the face of cynical smirks and painfully visible circumstances. If Abram was to be the father of faith for millennia to come, his faith had to be the kind that endures extraordinary tests. And the only way to endure them was to be put through them.

THE SIGN OF THE COVENANT

Circumcision was widely practiced in other cultures of Abraham's day, so it wasn't a Jewish invention or a novel concept. But in those cultures, it was always performed at the onset of puberty or as a preparation for marriage—in other words, at a time that was specifically associated with offspring. God moved Jewish circumcision to the eighth day of a boy's life. Why? Because an infant's life was considered viable after its first week; because eight often represents new beginnings in Scripture; and perhaps because in later law, the eighth day was when newborn animals became eligible for sacrifice (Lev. 22:27). In human terms, circumcision may have been an "offering" of a child to God—an act of dedication and a tangible mark for life.

Our faith has to endure tests too. We may never be promised a miracle as improbable as Abram's—though one could argue that the resurrection of the dead is just as faith-stretching—but if we seek to follow God, we will encounter plenty of challenges to our beliefs. That's by design. If we want the kind of faith that overcomes, we will have to encounter something to overcome. The question is, when we find ourselves caught between what we see with our eyes and what we know to be spiritually true, which will we choose to believe? That's the challenge of walking by faith, and every follower of God must learn to face it.

The Sign: Genesis 17

Focus: Genesis 17:1–21

Nearly thirteen years have passed since Ishmael was born, and Abram still has no son through Sarai. God appears to him again, and the specifics of the covenant are further refined. Abram will be the father not of a single nation but of many; the son will come through Sarai, even though she is ninety years old; the promise of many descendants and much land is an everlasting promise; and the time of fulfillment—that long-awaited day—will come within a year. But just as the promise is further spelled out, so are Abram's responsibilities. To this point, the only condition required of him was to go to the land God would show him. Now, for the first time, Abram is asked to respond. He is to serve God faithfully and live blamelessly, and he is to circumcise himself and all the males of his household. This mark of circumcision will be the sign of the everlasting covenant.

Abram doesn't understand, and he laughs at the thought. Why not fulfill the promise through Ishmael? Is it really wise—or even desirable—for an old couple to begin raising a child now? But God is insistent on the absurdity of his plan. He will indeed bless Ishmael, as he has already said. But this son, the son of promise, must come through Sarai.

In a huge turning point in the history of this promise, God announces one of his special names—*El Shaddai*, which means "God Almighty." He also changes the names of Abram and Sarai. They are each given an H, a twice-repeated letter in the covenant name of God (YHWH). Abram ("exalted father") becomes Abraham ("father of a multitude"), and Sarai ("princess") becomes Sarah, an alternate form of the same name. Their entire identity is now officially bound up in this covenant.

Discuss

- In light of all the interaction he and God already had regarding this promise, why do you think Abram was surprised that Sarai was the one through whom the child would come? What do you think he was expecting?

  _____
  _____
  _____
  _____

- Abram laughed when God spelled out his plans. Do you think Abram had given up on the promise? What attitude would you have toward God in the twenty-fourth year of waiting for him to fulfill a promise? Why?

  _____
  _____
  _____
  _____

Impossible? Genesis 18:1–15

The Lord appears to Abraham again, this time in the form of three men. In a flurry of hospitality, Abraham arranges rest, refreshment, and a banquet for his guests. Abraham stands with them as they eat under a tree, and the Lord initiates a conversation. "Where is Sarah?" he asks, and Abraham answers that she is in the nearby tent. The Lord reiterates the promise he gave Abraham in chapter 17, this time loud enough for Sarah to hear. Like Abraham, she laughs at the thought. "Is anything too hard for God?" says one of the men. Sarah denies her laughter, but it's futile to hide the truth from God. She did laugh. And the name of her son, already revealed to Abraham, will remind them both of their laughter for the rest of their lives. He will be called Isaac—"he laughs."

Discuss

- What "impossibilities" do you face today? If a messenger from the Lord came to you, what do you think he would say about your situation?

  _____

  _____

  _____

  _____

Interceding: Genesis 18:16–33

Abraham's favor in the sight of the Lord takes on added dimension once the three visitors finish their meal. God reveals his secret agenda to Abraham—a remarkable dynamic later captured in Amos 3:7—and invites his servant to intercede for

SACRED NAMING

Names were hugely significant in Hebrew Scripture. They had power. A person's personality and destiny were embedded in his or her name. Naming someone—as Adam named the animals, for example, or as parents gave their children prophetically significant names—was essentially an exercise of power over that person. So when God changed Abram and Sarai's names to Abraham and Sarah, he was establishing his supreme authority over their lives by giving them a change of identity and guaranteeing their destiny. This would have been seen by them and by every reader of Hebrew Scripture as a profound, life-changing event.

the sinful city in which Lot now lives. Abraham is tentative and respectful in his pleas, but he knows God well enough to appeal to his justice on behalf of the righteous rather than his judgment against the wicked. Abraham fears that he is testing the Lord, but in actuality the reverse is true. God is drawing his servant into a closer relationship in which plans are discussed, appeals are allowed, and friendships are formed. Abraham is invited to try and change God's mind.

This is what intercessors do—not because God needs to be redirected but because he wants his people to represent the world's needs to him. It's a repeated pattern in Scripture: God raises up those who will intercede in human affairs and bridge the gap between himself and the world. Ultimately, he sends the perfect Intercessor to stand in that gap forever (Isa. 59:16).

Discuss

- As a result of Abraham's intercession, God agrees to spare the city if ten righteous people are found. Though this number proves to be too high, the concept raises interesting questions: To what extent do the righteous preserve an entire community? Do you think God bases his dealings with a people or a nation primarily on the misdeeds of the unrighteous or on the deeds of the righteous? Why?

_____

_____

_____

_____

• Do you think your prayers can change God's mind? Why or why not?

_____

_____

_____

_____

A Case Study

Imagine: You know your society is in desperate condition and suffers from numerous social evils. It needs to be purified, and you know the only way for that to happen is for God to deal with its sins. But your country is also home to many thriving, influential ministries that are making a powerful impact for the kingdom of God around the world. If the country as a whole experiences judgment, these ministries will feel the effect. And if it doesn't, hearts probably won't turn back to the Lord. So when an angel of the Lord appears to you and invites you to plead your nation's case, you seriously weigh the consequences of your prayers.

- How will you plead? Should God deal kindly with your country for the sake of his servants within it, or should he deal harshly in order to alert people to their sins?
- How accurately do you think this situation represents your country today?
- In what ways have you seen God discipline a society? In what respects have you seen him withhold judgment? If you had to predict how he will deal with your country in the next ten years, what would you say?

Fulfillment

GENESIS 20–21

Euphoric protestors stood on the Berlin Wall in November 1989 and celebrated its official end while the world watched in fascination. Once-restricted citizens danced freely on a strip of land where people had often been shot for trying to flee. Long-separated loved ones hugged openly and visited each other's homes. A tightly controlled economy flourished with new commercial trade. On Christmas Day, Leonard Bernstein conducted Beethoven's "Ode to Joy" in a Berlin concert hall to celebrate the wall's collapse. A few months later, a who's who of rock stars performed the Pink Floyd rock opera "The Wall" on the remnants of the wall itself. It was an exhilarating time. The free world rejoiced over the evidence of communism crumbling.

People had waited decades for this moment, but few were prepared for its suddenness. After all, an East German leader had recently predicted that the wall would stand for another hundred years. Many who once believed that the wall was temporary had long since given up hope. It was a stone cold reality—literally. Unmovable, unyielding, unsympathetic. Until the day it fell.

The saying is true: "Hope deferred makes the heart sick, but a longing fulfilled is a tree of life" (Prov. 13:12). Ask anyone what their greatest longing is, and most people will be able to tell you without having to think about it. We harbor desires— deep, lasting yearnings of the heart—for fulfillment of one kind or another. Ultimately, we know our true fulfillment is in God himself, but we have plenty of dreams along the way. When we have to wait for them, hope seems to grow weaker. But when fulfillment comes, it feels like a tree of life.

A DAY TO REMEMBER

Rosh Hashanah, the Jewish New Year, is traditionally considered a celebration of the first day of creation. It's also the first of ten days of repentance, a time when God "takes account" of his people and when they look back over the last year and ask forgiveness for their sins. The period is considered a judicial examination of sorts, a yearly evaluation in which God measures each person and remembers his goodness and favor toward them. Because Genesis 21 contains both of these themes—the celebration of something new and God's taking note of someone (the literal translation of 21:1 is that God "took note" of Sarah)—this is the Torah portion read in synagogues every year on the first day of the year.

43

God knows all about your dreams and desires. He has even put some of them into your heart himself. It's true that many of them will only be fulfilled after a long wait, and some may have to be reshaped by his Spirit or replaced by something better. Though your heart ultimately finds its rest in him alone, he loves fulfilling your lesser desires from time to time. He knows the joy it brings.

Abraham's deep desire was finally met at the age of one hundred. That's a long time to wait, but the longer the wait, the sweeter the celebration. The mood of Abraham's life before chapter 21 is tense and uncomfortable, and before the chapter ends, there's another note of anguish. But for a brief moment in time, it's euphoric. Life is good. A promise has finally, finally been fulfilled. God's word has proven astoundingly true.

A Repeated Test: Genesis 20

There's a sense of déjà vu in Genesis 20. After all that Abraham and Sarah have been through, it seems that they would know not to pass off Sarah as his sister again. But the promise of a son now has an expiration date on it—God had designated the current year—and a king in southeastern Canaan, where the Philistines will one day dwell, might be a threat to the fulfillment. Perhaps Abraham's sense of self-preservation kicks in again, or maybe he trusts God to do what he did before. Regardless, he reverts to his standing policy; his wife—the soon-to-be mother of the promised son—is taken by a potentially hostile king.

God's protection is decisive, although he allows Sarah to remain in Abimelech's household long enough for the other women there to find out that they are infertile. God comes to the king in a dream and tells him the truth about Sarah.

Fortunately, he hasn't touched her yet, but he's furious over the lie he has been told. He turns her back over to Abraham—with parting gifts, just as a pharaoh had done years before—and catastrophe is averted. Abraham, now the first person in Scripture designated as a prophet, prays for Abimelech's household. Once again, God has zealously protected his promise and his plan.

Discuss

- Why do you think Abraham traveled to a new place and repeated the events of chapter 12 again?

  _____

  _____

  _____

  _____

- What does God's response tell us about his zeal for his own purposes? Do you think he watches over his plans for your life with the same kind of zeal? Why or why not?

  _____

  _____

  _____

  _____

Celebration and Sadness: Genesis 21

Focus: Genesis 21:1–21

Faith, patience, and perseverance. According to Hebrews 6:12 and 10:35–36, that's what it takes to inherit a promise. Abraham's faith, patience, and perseverance are finally rewarded as the son of laughter is born. The first two verses emphasize God's faithfulness in the process: "as he had said . . . the Lord did for Sarah what he had promised . . . at the very time God had promised him." Abraham keeps his part of the covenant too; he circumcises his son on the eighth day.

Some two to three years later, Isaac is weaned and Abraham throws a party. It's a great celebration until Sarah sees the teenage Ishmael laughing at her son. It's a play on the son of laughter's name—Ishmael is literally "Isaac-ing" him. Is he taunting or mocking, resentful at all the fuss being made over his little half-sibling? Or is he genuinely having a good time, fitting in much too well as the older brother and making Sarah uncomfortable? Either way, she's offended—so much so that she can't even speak their names when she orders Abraham to banish Hagar and Ishmael. There can be no rivals to her son's inheritance, regardless of laws and customs forbidding harsh treatment of children of a surrogate. She wants "that slave woman and her son" out of her sight forever.

Abraham is grieved. He loves Ishmael and had once even urged God to make him the son of promise (17:18). But God assures Abraham that he is watching over the boy. Once again Hagar is sent into the wilderness, and once again God provides for her. Ishmael is fading—perhaps he has given his mother the greater share of water—but God leads them to a well where they can drink. They make a home in the desert, Ishmael becomes an archer, and his Egyptian mother finds him an Egyptian wife. Through him, a great nation is being formed.

Discuss

- Why do you think Sarah reacted so harshly to Ishmael's treatment of Isaac? Why do you think God compelled

Abraham to heed her orders instead of insisting that Ishmael stay?

_____

_____

_____

_____

* In what areas of your life is God currently requiring faith, patience, and perseverance? What result do you expect as an outcome of those attitudes?

_____

_____

_____

_____

A CASE STUDY

Imagine: Long ago, God placed a dream in your heart—well, you're 99 percent sure it was him—and you've held onto it ever since. By human standards, the odds are against it; your visible circumstances keep reminding you that it probably can't be done. So do your "concerned" friends. But you aren't dealing with a God who is subject to the odds, so you've kept the faith. At several points in your life, your dream has seemed to come close to reality, only to slip back again into the "maybe one day" recesses of your heart. Your hopes have been built up and then dashed so many times that you're almost afraid to hope anymore.

* In what ways are you likely to second-guess yourself? Do you wonder whether your dream was really from God?

47

Whether you somehow blew your shot at it along the way? Whether God is really able or willing to deliver on his promise? All of the above?

- How long do you hold on before you finally give up? What criteria would you use to determine whether you should give up?

- How would you feel about God in the process? How would you feel about him on the day your dream is fulfilled?

An Epic Test

GENESIS 22–23, 25:1–11

The artist chose his colors carefully, composed his elements precisely, and painted a highly symbolic depiction of his own heart. It was strange but compelling, intriguing but obscure, hard to look at but also hard to look away. Many who saw the masterpiece in the gallery never understood its symbolism—a heart is hard to portray, after all—but some did. Everyone, however, could tell that it was skillfully done. And even those who didn't quite understand it could still see something of the artist's heart. It was revealing even in its mystery.

The artist in this description is God, and his painting is the *Akedah*—or the binding of Isaac, as it is more familiarly known. God told his faithful servant who had waited so long for a promised son to take that son up on a mountain and sacrifice him. It's

49

a prophetic portrait of God's purposes, though the participants in this real-life drama had no idea what it pointed to as they were going through it. Abraham could not have known he was playing the part of another Father who would sacrifice his only Son one day. Isaac could not have known that his submission to this shocking act would point to a certain Savior who would later give up his own life without a fight. The ram whose horns were caught in a thicket—of thorns, no doubt—was symbolic of another sacrificial Lamb centuries later.

All the elements of the later story were there: a three-day journey; a hill called Moriah on which a city named Jerusalem would one day be built; a sacrificial son carrying his own wood; the Jewish name of the event (*Akedah*) derived from the son's "stripes" or wounds; a virtual resurrection when the son is given back to the father. In many ways the sacrifice of Isaac points to the Passover events when Israel left Egypt; but even more so it points to a Savior on a cross nearly two millennia later. By a Master Artist's hand, Abraham and his son painted a picture that only future generations would see. But all they knew was that God was asking them to do something harder than they had ever done before.

Abraham's story isn't the only time God painted a picture in the lives of his people. Many of the stories in Hebrew Scripture point to the life and ministry of the Messiah. Many of its people—Moses, Ruth, and David, for example—played out messianic prophecies without even knowing it. God often illustrated spiritual truths in the lives of his prophets. For example, Hosea marries a prostitute to demonstrate God's faithfulness in the face of Israel's unfaithfulness and Ezekiel's wife dies to illustrate the tearless grief of God. If all the world's a stage, as Shakespeare once wrote, then God has used it for quite a few divine dramas.

50

HINENI

The phrase "Here I am"—*hineni*, in Hebrew—is used only a handful of times in Scripture, but when it's spoken in response to God, it's almost always followed by a landmark, history-changing event. Abraham uses it twice in Genesis 22: first when God calls his name to tell him to sacrifice Isaac and again when the angel calls his name to stop him. Jacob answers God's call twice with "Here I am": once when God told him to move back to Canaan and once when God told him to move the family to Egypt. It's how Samuel and Isaiah answered their initial calls and how David responds to God in Psalm 40:7, which is then applied to the Messiah in Hebrews 10:7. In every case, God does a major work in response. The message is clear: God greatly uses those who are ready and available for him to use.

God continues to stage his drama in our lives today, as many people can attest. Sometimes life looks confusing from ground level, but the heart of the Father may be revealed as we look back on the big picture. The problem is that we usually have to go through our trials without seeing how they fit into the big picture. All we have to go on is our faith that God is working on our behalf and our trust that his ways are good. Sometimes that's all that gets us through dark times. And sometimes it looks like those dark times are arranged by a hand that isn't exactly on our side.

Abraham could have assumed from such a difficult command that God had turned against him, or decided that in the long run the cost of serving God exceeded the benefits, or anything else we're tempted to feel when we're in a crisis. But he didn't. He simply trusted that God knew what he was doing and would make it right in the end. In response to his trust, he found that God is trustworthy. Abraham passed his most

51

arduous test, and the portrait the Master painted through his life is today considered an eternal masterpiece.

The Binding of Isaac: Genesis 22

Focus: Genesis 22:1–19

It's one of the most staggering episodes in the Bible, excruciatingly sparse in its details and extremely uncomfortable to read. We can hardly imagine what goes through Abraham's head when he's told to sacrifice Isaac, but imagine is all we can do. The text doesn't tell us anything other than the external facts. Apparently Abraham asks no questions, even though years ago he had openly argued with God about Sodom. He suggests no alternatives, even though he has a long history of suggesting alternative plans to God. The absurdity of this request exceeds even the absurdity of the original promise, yet there's no hint of reluctance on Abraham's part. No wrestling, no pleas, no anxiety, no long talks with Sarah about what must be done. In fact, he leaves early the next morning, perhaps to avoid a conversation about it. It's only a three-day trip to the hills of Moriah, but in many ways it's the longest journey of Abraham's life.

What's the purpose of such a brutal command? It was common for pagans to offer such sacrifices to their gods; is God challenging Abraham's devotion to see if he's as committed as they are? Is he testing to see if he really is Abraham's "great reward" (15:1), almost daring him to focus on the gift rather than the Giver? Is he simply demonstrating a truth that Abraham's descendants will find all too familiar—that a covenant with God comes at a painful cost? No reason is given, at least not until after the dreadful event. Though God seems alarmingly contradictory—this is the *only* son of promise through whom those multitudes of descendants will supposedly come—Abraham must simply carry out his instructions.

Abraham gets near the designated spot and leaves his servants behind. "We will worship and return to you," he tells them. Is he covering his secret or making a statement of faith? The writer of Hebrews will one day conclude the latter (Heb. 11:17–19), but Genesis 22 doesn't get that specific. The father and son journey up this mountain, the place where Jerusalem will one day be built and another Son will be sacrificed, and together they prepare the altar. Still, Isaac doesn't know his father's will. But he soon finds out, and apparently he complies. He's at least a teenager now, if not older (a *na'ar*, a "young man," in verses 5 and 12) and his father is very old. Isaac can resist if he wants to, but there's no hint that he does. He is a picture of willing submission.

An angel stops the sacrifice, of course, and God provides another—a ram caught by its horns. Once again God reiterates his covenant terms with Abraham. This time he is even more emphatic than ever. Because of Abraham's obedience, God will bless him with all the things he has already promised. Why now? Have God's promises been tentative until this deciding event? No, but God has known about this

A UNIQUE WOMAN

Sarah is the only woman in the Bible to have her name changed and the only woman to have her age at death recorded. Both are significant, implying that this matriarch has the status of a patriarch in a highly patriarchal society. If Abraham is the father of faith, Sarah is the mother—a miraculous example of what God can do through those who believe.

event all along. He has known Abraham's heart in advance and made his promises accordingly. Now it's clear to Abraham and Isaac too: this is the kind of faith on which eternal kingdoms are built.

There's no record of what Abraham and Isaac talk about on the way back down the mountain, of the nature of their relationship thereafter, or of how (or whether) Sarah is ever told what happened. Some rabbis speculate that it devastated her—her death is the next story told, and she and Abraham aren't in the same household when she dies. Whether that's a telling picture or not, God has clearly put his chosen family through a lot of stress. But in the long run, the benefits of being chosen will far exceed the costs.

Discuss

- How would you respond to God if he gave you a promise and then seemed to retract it?

  _____

  _____

  _____

  _____

- How clearly do you think God would have to speak to convince you of such a strange and dreadful command? If you were Sarah, how would you have responded to Abraham's conviction that this is what God wanted him to do?

  _____

  _____

  _____

  _____

- Have you had to obey God when you didn't understand why? How is that a greater example of faith than obeying when you do understand?

_____

_____

_____

_____

After the Test: Genesis 23; 25:1–11

Focus: Genesis 23:1–9; 25:1–11

In the two previous chapters, Abraham has had to be willing to sacrifice two sons—sending Ishmael into the wilderness and offering Isaac on an altar, both by God's command. Has he questioned whether he really wants to follow this God? Seemingly not; he lives out his days faithfully and relatively uneventfully. As far as we know, God never speaks to Abraham again after the incident on Moriah. From this point on, his story is primarily about arranging his affairs—burying Sarah, finding a wife for Isaac, remarrying, and filling the region with other sons who will also have many descendants.

In buying land for Sarah's grave, Abraham legally possesses his first piece of the land of promise, however small it may be. Over time, it will grow. And his family grows too. Long ago considered by his wife to be too old to have a child, he now has six more sons. He lives long enough to see them grow into adulthood, give them gifts, and send them into the east. But the inheritance belongs to only one: the son of promise.

Isaac and Ishmael reunite one last time—to bury their father upon his death at the age of 175. Abraham's lifelong test of faith is over. For countless generations to come, his covenant is securely in God's hands.

55

Discuss

- Romans 4:20 says that Abraham "did not waver through unbelief regarding the promise of God." Though this is undoubtedly God's overall assessment of his faith, in what ways have we seen hints of "wavering"? In what sense is the big picture of his life a picture of steady growth in faith?

  _____

  _____

  _____

  _____

A CASE STUDY

Imagine: Your normally routine life is interrupted one night by a dramatic vision in which God offers you an amazing choice. You have been chosen as a vehicle to bless all the kingdoms of the world for eternity to come, and you will be richly rewarded for your service. Your name will go down in history, and people will look to you as a model of faith—but only after you're gone. While you're alive, you'll have God's presence and some material blessings, but you'll face torturous decisions, bear the weight of enormous responsibility, be looked at with suspicion, and suffer painful losses. The costs will be staggering, but the rewards more so. There are no hard feelings if you decline; the choice is up to you.

- Would you accept God's offer, even with all the costs spelled out ahead of time? Which is more appealing to you: great benefits at great costs, or a less up-and-down, more comfortable existence? Why?

- To what extent do you think this is a choice for every believer? In what ways is it unique only to Abraham?
- Do you think Abraham would have chosen his life if he had known ahead of time what it would involve? Why or why not?

Conclusion

Abraham's legacy is vast. Jews, Christians, and Muslims—well over half of the world's population—all consider him the father of their faith. The extravagant promises first given in Genesis 12—then repeated in chapters 13, 15, 17, and 28; and in 1 Chronicles 16:16–19; Acts 3:25; and Galatians 3:8—were recorded before they were proven true, but have since been proven true in the extreme. He *has* become a great nation, a father of many nations, the ancestor of descendants too numerous to count. God has kept his word.

The New Testament emphasizes Abraham more as a spiritual father than as a physical ancestor. Paul describes it most clearly:

> The promise comes by faith, so that it may be by grace and may be guaranteed to all Abraham's offspring—not only to those who are of the law but also to those who are of the faith of Abraham. He is the father of us all. As it is written: "I have made you a father of many nations." He is our father in the sight of God, in whom he believed.
>
> Romans 4:16–17

> Consider Abraham: "He believed God, and it was credited to him as righteousness." Understand, then, that those who believe are children of Abraham. The Scripture foresaw that God would justify

the Gentiles by faith, and announced the gospel in advance to Abraham: "All nations will be blessed through you." So those who have faith are blessed along with Abraham, the man of faith.

Galatians 3:6–9

In other words, God's promises to Abraham belong to anyone who believes in Abraham's seed: that is, Jesus. "If you belong to Christ, then you are Abraham's seed, and heirs according to the promise" (Gal. 3:29). Through Jesus, the Abrahamic covenant has been fulfilled.

But there are aspects of the Abrahamic covenant that have not yet been fulfilled. Not "all the peoples of the earth" have been blessed by him (Gen. 12:3). The faith that comes from Abraham is still unknown to many. The Messiah that came through him and those who follow the Messiah are still fulfilling that mission. The Abrahamic covenant is still at work in the world.

Meanwhile, we are to live as Abraham lived—by faith. We are to live as strangers and sojourners in a world that is not our ultimate home. We are to embrace the promises God gives us and hold on to them with patience and perseverance, never compromising them and never settling for second-best substitutes. We are to offer our hearts' desires on the altar and trust that God will raise them up again in his way and in his time. And we are, like Abraham, to be "looking forward to the city with foundations, whose architect and builder is God" (Heb. 11:10).

God is a God of covenant, and he fulfills his word. Just as he called Abraham into a relationship with him, so he calls us. Abraham became a friend of God through his faithfulness to the covenant—a lasting legacy that has become our inheritance. If we believe, we receive the same blessings given to this patriarch of faith. By faith, we too find ourselves in a relationship with a God who fulfills his word.

Leader's Notes

Session 1

Genesis 12:1–9, first discussion question. It may help to point out that Abram will eventually be known as the "father" or prototype of faith in the Bible. It's only fitting that his initial experience with God hinges entirely on trusting what can't be seen.

Genesis 12:10–20, second set of questions. If the discussion doesn't move naturally in this direction, help group members make the connection between Abram's experience and their own—that even when we don't make all the right choices, God still watches our backs.

Session 2

Genesis 14, first discussion question and Case Study. Centuries after Abram, in the painful years between the time that David was anointed king and the time he could actually assume the throne, David had two opportunities to kill King Saul and achieve God's promise. Yet, like Abram, he refused (see 1 Samuel 24:1–11 and 26:7–24). Likewise, Satan gave Jesus the opportunity to receive the kingdoms of the world, just as God promised (see Psalm 2:7–8 and Matthew 4:8–9). But Jesus also refused to accomplish God's promise in the wrong way and at the wrong time. These are clearer cases of right and wrong than Abram's was. His victory might have looked as if it were God's means of giving him the land. Somehow, Abram discerned that it wasn't. This scriptural principle can make for a very interesting discussion. Participants may be able to share examples from their own lives of having the right opportunity at the wrong time or in the wrong way.

Session 3

Genesis 15, first discussion question. This particular covenant—and one might argue that many of God's covenants are like this—is entirely up to God to fulfill. Because God sealed it unilaterally, Abram can do nothing to fulfill it or to disqualify himself from it. It's a done deal. Your group may want to discuss how or whether this covenant represents the cross of Christ and our salvation by grace through faith. In what sense is salvation a unilateral initiative of God? In what sense is it conditional on human response? If your members come from varying theological backgrounds, this could turn into a lively but fruitful discussion.

Genesis 16, discussion questions. This was a real dilemma for Abram and Sarai, and it's a real dilemma for us. Faith almost always requires some sort of action in Scripture. For example, the Jordan River miraculously opened for the Israelites, but they had to step into the water first; the walls of Jericho miraculously fell down, but the Israelites had to march around them and shout first; and so on. So it's reasonable to think that we need to do our part when God has given a promise. On the other hand, many promises require a lot of waiting, and God doesn't respond to our attempts to force the issue. Case in point: Abram and Sarai. Group members can probably share plenty of examples from their own lives of when they didn't know whether to move forward or passively wait for God to act. (And sometimes the latter requires greater faith.) The discussion should take into account the fact that the tension between these two approaches is real, and both are biblical. The hard part is knowing which approach to take in a given situation. The best biblical solution seems to be to wait unless given specific instructions to act. But discerning those instructions is a real challenge.

Session 4

Genesis 18:1–15, discussion questions. If your group is in the habit of sharing prayer requests, some of them will immediately come to mind with these questions. Because we often pray without really thinking about how God might respond, discussing some of the ways he might answer—including both the miraculous and the mundane—can serve to strengthen faith that he will.

Genesis 18:16–33, discussion questions and Case Study. There are two sides to this issue. For helpful background, compare and contrast Jeremiah 5:1 and Ezekiel 14:12–20. The first emphasizes God's desire to save an entire city based on the righteousness of one of its citizens. The second indicates that God sometimes judges an entire country even when its citizens include his choicest servants. In one case, his mercy is swayed by a minority; in the other, it isn't.

Session 6

Genesis 23; 25:1–11, discussion questions. Though Paul's statement about Abraham never wavering seems to be an idealized picture—after all, Abraham at times asked questions of doubt, offered alternative plans, and laughed at God's specific fulfillment—it actually highlights a very encouraging principle. Though we struggle in our faith, stumble from time to time, and experience the ups and downs between belief and doubt, God bases his assessment on how we ended. Did we end with faith? Then faith endured, regardless of the path we took along the way. If God applies this "big picture" perspective to Abraham, he applies it to us as well.

Bibliography

Berlin, Adele, Marc Zvi Brettler, and Michael Fishbane, eds. *The Jewish Study Bible*. Oxford and New York: Oxford University Press, 2004.

First Fruits of Zion. *Torah Club, Volume 2: Shadows of the Messiah*. Marshfield, MO: First Fruits of Zion, 1994–2004.

Fox, Everett. *The Schocken Bible, vol. 1: The Five Books of Moses*. New York: Schocken Books, 1995.

Hoerth, Alfred J. *Archaeology and the Old Testament*. Grand Rapids: Baker, 1998.

Kaiser, Walter C., Jr., and Duane Garrett, eds. *Archaeological Study Bible*. Grand Rapids: Zondervan, 2006.

Keller, Werner. *The Bible as History*. New York: William Morrow and Company, 1981.

Morris, Henry M. *The Genesis Record: A Scientific and Devotional Commentary on the Book of Beginnings*. Grand Rapids: Baker, 1976.

Schorsch, Ismar. *Canon Without Closure: Torah Commentaries*. New York: Aviv Press, 2007.

Shanks, Herschel, ed. *Ancient Israel: From Abraham to the Roman Destruction of the Temple*. Upper Saddle River, NJ: Prentice Hall, 1999.

Telushkin, Joseph. *Biblical Literacy: The Most Important People, Events, and Ideas of the Hebrew Bible*. New York: William Morrow, 1997.

Walton, John H., Victor H. Matthews, and Mark W. Chavalas. *The IVP Bible Background Commentary: Old Testament*. Downers Grove, IL: InterVarsity Press, 2000.

**WALK
THRU THE
BIBLE®**

Helping people everywhere
live God's Word

For more than three decades, Walk Thru the Bible has created disciple-ship materials and cultivated leadership networks that together are reaching millions of people through live seminars, print publications, audiovisual curricula, and the Internet. Known for innovative methods and high-quality resources, we serve the whole body of Christ across denominational, cultural, and national lines. Through our strong and cooperative international partnerships, we are strategically positioned to address the church's greatest need: developing mature, committed, and spiritually reproducing believers.

Walk Thru the Bible communicates the truths of God's Word in a way that makes the Bible readily accessible to anyone. We are committed to developing user-friendly resources that are Bible centered, of excellent quality, life changing for individuals, and catalytic for churches, ministries, and movements; and we are committed to maintaining our global reach through strategic partnerships while adhering to the highest levels of in-tegrity in all we do.

Walk Thru the Bible partners with the local church worldwide to fulfill its mission, helping people "walk thru" the Bible with greater clarity and understanding. Live seminars and small group curricula are taught in over 45 languages by more than 80,000 people in more than 70 countries, and more than 100 million devotionals have been packaged into daily maga-zines, books, and other publications that reach over five million people each year.

Walk Thru the Bible
4201 North Peachtree Road
Atlanta, GA 30341-1207
770-458-9300
www.walkthru.org